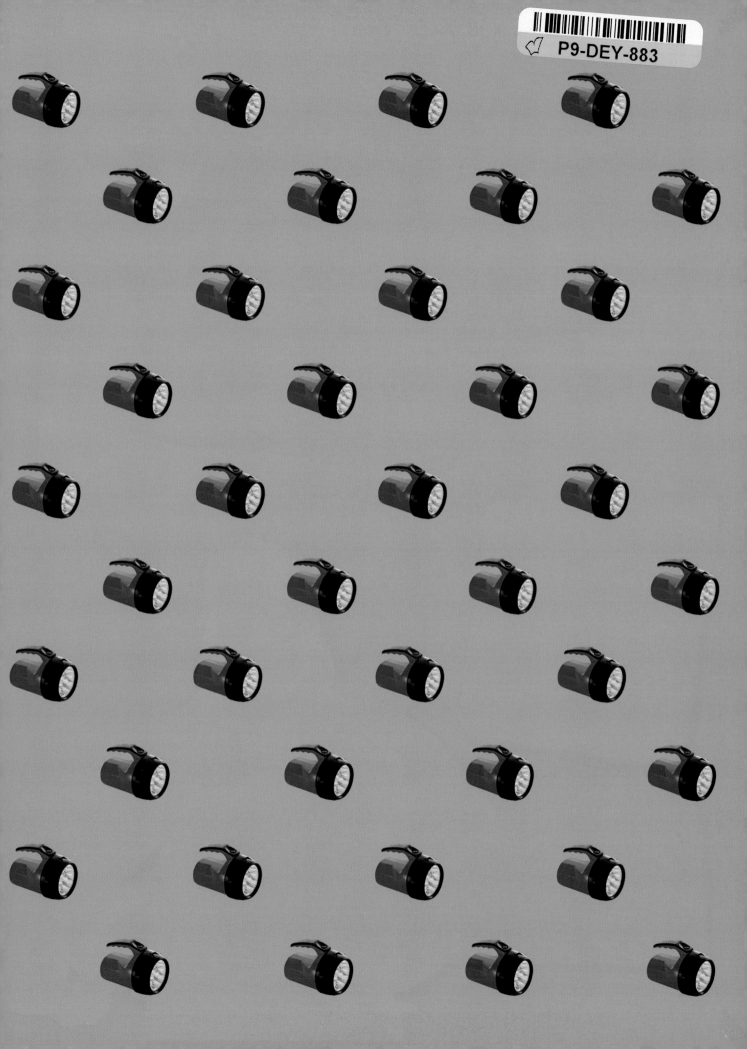

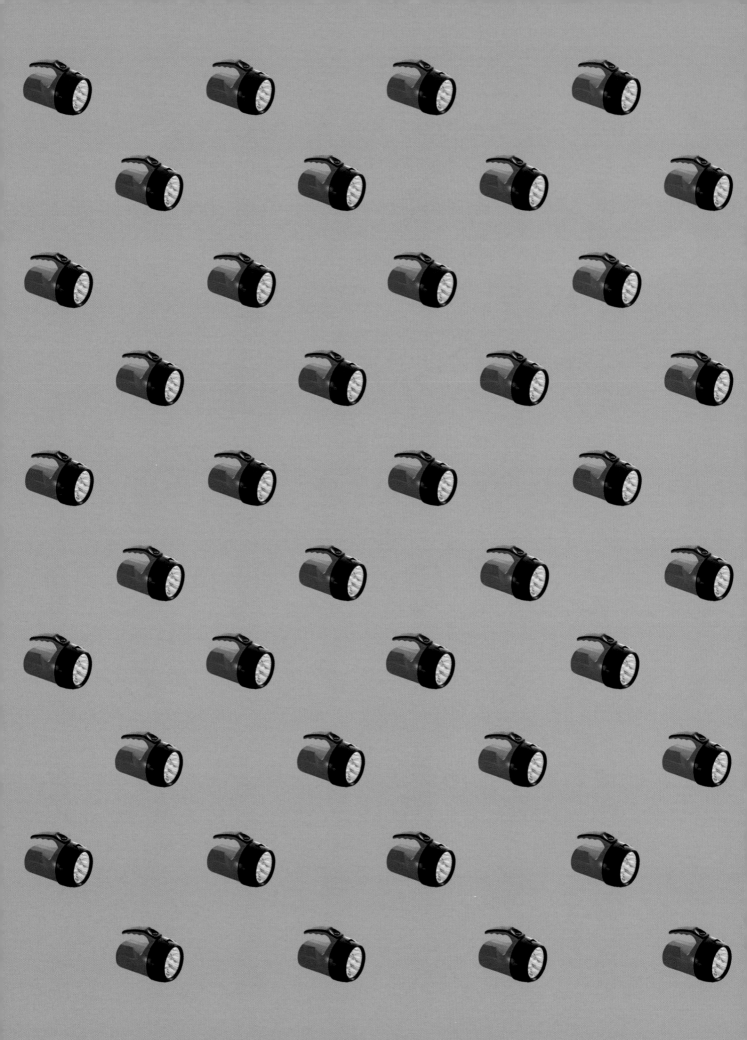

one-stop science

Experiments with a Flashlight

By Angela Royston

A⁺

Smart Apple Media

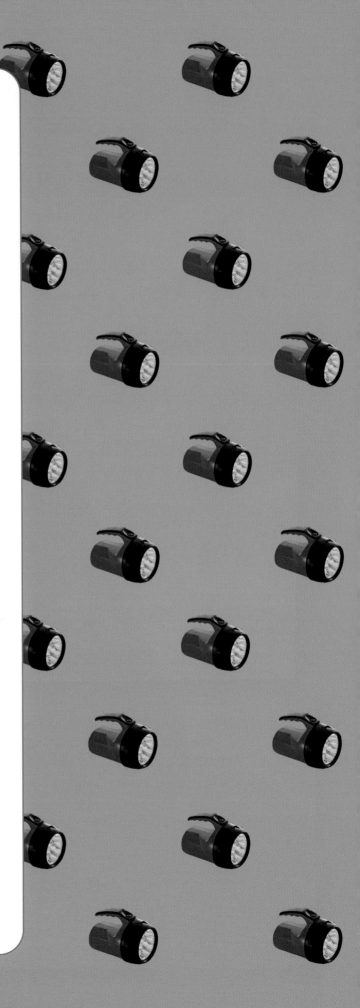

Published by Smart Apple Media,
an imprint of Black Rabbit Books
P.O. Box 3263, Mankato, Minnesota 56002
www.smartapplemedia.com

Cataloging-in-Publication Data is available from
the Library of Congress
ISBN: 978-1-62588- 141-0 (library binding)
ISBN: 978-1-68071-017-5 (eBook)

Series editor: Sarah Peutrill
Art director: Jonathan Hair
Design: Matt Lilly and Ruth Walton
Science consultant: Meredith Blakeney
Photographs: Paul Bricknell, unless
otherwise credited
Models: Rianna Aniakor, Yusuf Hofri, Samuel
Knudsen, India May Nugent, Lyia Sheikh

Credits: Ashley Cooper/Alamy: 6b. Marc
Dietrich/Shutterstock: 7c. Artem
Illarionov/Shutterstock: 7cl. Tom King/Alamy:
7t. Kokhanchikov/Shutterstock: 11b.
LampLighterSDV/Shutterstock: 19b. Matt Lilly:
23b, 25b. magicinfoto/Shutterstock: 21b.
moodboard/Alamy: 6c. Shaun Robinson/
Shutterstock: 27b. Pedro Salaverria/
Shutterstock: 8c. Kippy Spilker/Shutterstock:
17b. Tuna Tirkaz/istockphoto: 6t. Alaettin
Yildirm/Shutterstock: 7cr. Every attempt has
been made to clear copyright. Should there be
any inadvertent omission please apply to the
publisher for rectification.

Published by arrangement with Franklin Watts,
London.

Printed in the United States of America by CG
Book Printers, North Mankato, Minnesota.

PO1777
3-2016

Contents

What is a Flashlight? 6

Taking a Flashlight Apart 8

Make Your Own Circuit 9

Light Travels in Straight Lines 10

Making Shadows 12

Exploring Shadows 14

Bouncing Light 16

Making Light Bend 18

Making Colored Light 20

Mixing Colored Lights 22

Make a Rainbow 24

What Makes the Sky Turn Red? 26

Glossary 28

Further Information 29

Index 30

Words in **bold** are in the glossary on page 28.

What is a Flashlight?

A flashlight is a **device** that makes light. It contains **batteries** that produce **electricity** to light up the **bulb**. Flashlights are small and lightweight and are easy to carry around.

Flashlights are particularly useful for seeing outdoors at night. Campers use them in their tents and around the campsite. Security guards and the police use them to search dark and shadowy places.

◄ A flashlight gives a single beam of light. Some flashlights give a stronger light than other flashlights.

Kinds of flashlights

Flashlights are different shapes, depending on how they are used. A headlamp is fixed to a headband. It points exactly where you are looking and leaves both of your hands free. **Spelunkers**, for example, use headlamps to explore caves and tunnels underground.

▲ Spelunkers often have to crawl along narrow, dark tunnels. A headlamp is the best kind of flashlight to light their way.

On your bike

Cycle lights are a kind of flashlight, too. Cyclists should have cycle lights fitted to the front and back of their bicycles. Some cycle lights flash on and off so the drivers of motor vehicles can see them more easily.

◄ When it is dark, cycle lights help other people to see the cyclist.

LED flashlights

Most flashlights use a bulb that is a smaller version of a traditional light bulb. An LED flashlight uses a light emitting diode, which gives a brighter light than a traditional bulb. It also uses less energy, which means the batteries last longer.

▲ Flashlights vary in size as well as shape. Bigger flashlights use more powerful batteries than smaller flashlights.

The experiments in this book use a flashlight to explore light, **shadows,** and other aspects of science including electricity. They will work best in a dimly lit room, using a powerful flashlight that gives a strong light.

Taking a Flashlight Apart

Flashlights need electricity to work. Most have batteries that produce the electricity, but the batteries have to be in the correct position for the electricity to flow.

You will need:
A flashlight that works

1

Find out how to turn the flashlight on and off. Take out the batteries and examine them. Each one has a plus sign and a minus sign.

2 Put the batteries back in the flashlight and turn it on. Try turning each battery first one way around and then the other. Make a note of the positions of the plus and minus ends each time. How many ways can you get the flashlight to work?

What happened?

The bulb lit up when electricity traveled from the batteries through the flashlight and bulb and back to the batteries. Electricity needs an unbroken path, called a circuit, to flow through. The circuit is only completed when the plus end of one battery is connected to the minus end of the other battery.

Make Your Own Circuit

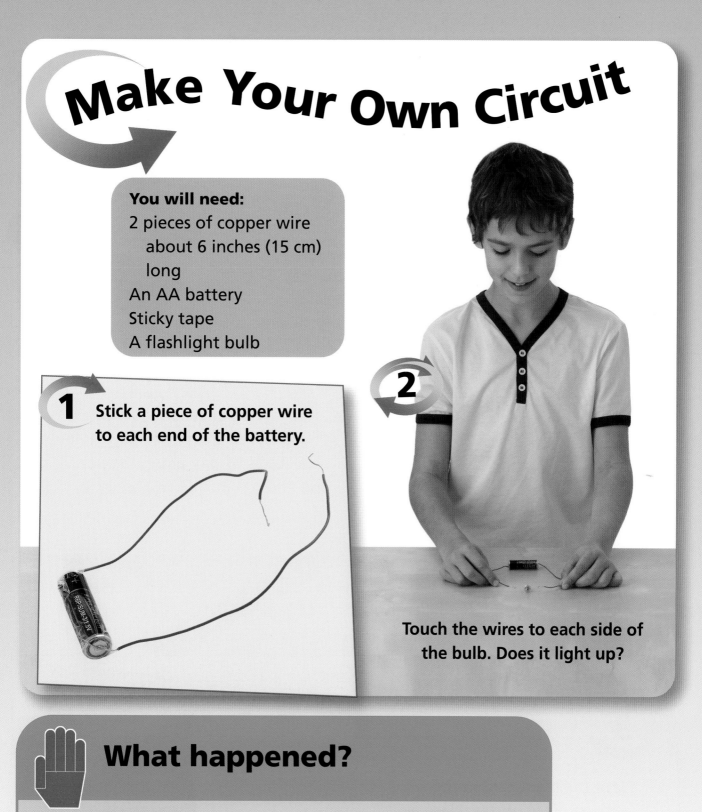

You will need:
2 pieces of copper wire
 about 6 inches (15 cm)
 long
An AA battery
Sticky tape
A flashlight bulb

1 Stick a piece of copper wire to each end of the battery.

2

Touch the wires to each side of the bulb. Does it light up?

What happened?

When the wires touched the bulb, they completed the circuit. Electricity from the battery flowed through the bulb and lit it up. Electricity always flows in the same direction, from the plus end of the battery to the minus end.

Light Travels in Straight Lines

Light does not bend around shapes like sound does. Light always travels in a straight line. This flashlight experiment proves it!

You will need:
A flashlight
3 notecards
A piece of printer paper
A large nail
Modeling clay
A black card
Paper, pencil, and ruler

1 Hold the notecards so the bottom edges are on top of each other. Make a hole through the middle using the nail.

2 Draw a pencil line down the center of the paper. Lay three small balls of clay along the pencil line about 1 inch (3 cm) apart.

3 Place the black card in the farthest piece of clay. Place a notecard in each of the other two pieces, so the hole in the notecard is above the line on the paper.

4 Shine the flashlight through the hole in the first notecard. Tilt the flashlight slightly until the circle of light hits the hole in the second notecard. Can you see the light on the black card? Turn the flashlight a little to the left. What happens?

5 Add the third card in front of the other cards. Can you still get the beam to hit the black card?

6 Take away the notecard nearest the black card. Now take away the next notecard. What happens to the spot of light?

What happened?

When the holes were lined up in a straight line, the beam traveled straight through them. The bigger the gap between the last hole and the black screen, the larger the final circle of light. This is because the light spreads out.

◀ The light from this old film projector spreads out to fill the screen.

Making Shadows

When light hits an object, a shadow forms behind it. Find out what different shadows you can make with various objects, including your hands.

You will need:
A flashlight
A mug
Building blocks
A white wall or screen
A transparent plastic bottle

1 Hold the mug about 1.5 inches (4 cm) from the wall or screen, and shine the flashlight on it. What shape is the shadow?

2 Do you think that something that is transparent will create a shadow? Shine the flashlight onto the plastic bottle and see if you are right.

3 Make a stack of blocks. Shine the flashlight onto the stack. What happens to the shadow when you change the arrangement of the stack?

What happened?

When light hits an object, some of the light is blocked but the rest travels on in straight lines past the object. Thus, the space behind the object is less well lit than the space around it. This forms a shadow that is exactly the same shape as the object.

Making Shapes

Use your hands to make these shapes. Ask a friend to shine the flashlight on your hands to make the shadows. What shapes are the shadows? What other shapes can you make?

Exploring Shadows

Find out how the position of an object can change the size and shape of its shadow.

You will need:
A flashlight
An object, such as a small plastic figure
A table
A white wall or screen
Ruler, paper, and pencil

1 Place the figure on the table 4 inches (10 cm) from the screen. Place the flashlight on the table 12 inches (30 cm) from the screen and shine it on the figure. Measure the height of the shadow and write it down.

2 Now move the figure, so it is 6 inches (15 cm) from the screen. Measure the height of the shadow again. Repeat with the figure 8 inches (20 cm) from the screen.

3 Make a graph to show how the size of the shadow changes as the figure is moved away from the screen.

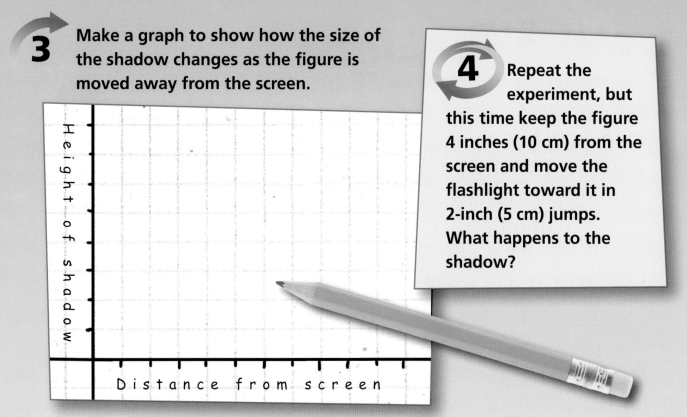

Height of shadow

Distance from screen

4 Repeat the experiment, but this time keep the figure 4 inches (10 cm) from the screen and move the flashlight toward it in 2-inch (5 cm) jumps. What happens to the shadow?

changing shape

Keep the figure on the table, but change the height of the flashlight. Start with the flashlight 12 inches (30 cm) behind the figure and 12 inches (30 cm) above the table. Slowly lower the flashlight, but keep it shining on the figure. What happens to the shadow?

The sun
The height of the sun in the sky changes during the day. Measure the height and direction of the shadow of a stick (stuck upright in the ground) at different times during the day. How do you think sundials work?

Bouncing Light

When light hits an object, some of it bounces off. Some surfaces **reflect** light better than others. This experiment will work best in a dark or dim room.

You will need:
A flashlight
A mirror

1 Shine the flashlight into the mirror and look for the reflection of the light on the wall. Where do you think the reflected light will be if you angle the flashlight to the left?

2 Angle the flashlight to the left. Was your prediction correct? Now predict where the light will be when you angle the beam to the right, then up, and then down. Test your predictions.

What happened?

Light travels in straight lines, so when it hit the mirror at an angle, it was reflected at an angle. Light is only reflected straight back to you when you point it straight at the mirror.

Testing other surfaces

Collect some shiny objects such as a shiny, flat top, a can of food, a piece of metal foil, and a mirror. Shine the flashlight on each object. Which reflects light the best? Which one reflects the least?

Reflectors

Reflector strips, like those used on safety jackets, help make people easier to see at night. Reflector strips use glass beads that work like tiny mirrors to reflect car lights and other lights.

◀ Firefighters wear clothes with reflective strips, so they can be seen in the dark.

Making Light Bend

Light always travels in straight lines—or does it? This flashlight experiment works best in a dimly lit or dark room.

You will need:
A flashlight
A small, clear plastic bottle
Metal foil
A colored plastic bowl
A pitcher of water

1 Wrap the metal foil around the side of the bottle. Make sure the top and bottom are not covered.

2 Fill the bottle with water. Press the flashlight against the bottom of the bottle and turn it on.

3 Hold the flashlight firmly against the bottle as you slowly pour the water into the bowl. Can you see a patch of light at the bottom of the bowl? Look closely at the water flowing between the bottle and the bowl. Can you see the beam of light bending with the water?

What happened?

The light looks as if it is bending, but it is being reflected from side to side inside the stream of water.

Fiber optics

This experiment shows how fiber optics works. An optical fiber is a narrow glass tube that carries signals in the form of light. It is used, for example, to carry telephone signals and works much better than the traditional method of passing electrical signals along a metal wire.

▶ Each of these fiber optic cables can carry up to 10 million signals at the same time.

Making Colored Light

This experiment shows you how to make different colored lights and explores how color **filters** work.

You will need:
A flashlight
3 clear, square plastic water
 bottles, about a third filled
 with water
Red, blue, and green food dyes
A sheet of white paper

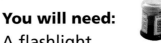

1 Add a few drops of red dye to the first bottle.

2 Hold the paper behind the bottle and shine the flashlight through the colored water. What color is the patch of light?

3 Add a few drops of blue dye to the second bottle and a few drops of green dye to the third bottle.
What color do you think the light patch will be for each?
Were you right?

4 Put the red water in front of the blue water. What color do you think the patch will be now? Were you right? What happens with different combinations of colored water?

Filters that are pure red, blue, and green give the best results. Food dyes have other colors mixed with them, so they may not cut out the light completely.

What happened?

The red water acted as a red filter, which allowed only red light to pass through it. Similarly, the blue filter allowed only blue light through and the green filter allowed only green light through. So when you shined the light through two different colored filters, no light reached the paper!

Filters on stage

Color filters are used by lighting experts to create exciting effects on stage for concerts and plays.

Mixing Colored Lights

When you mix red and blue paints, you get purple. What happens when you mix red and blue lights?

You will need:
3 flashlights
Red, blue, and green filters
Sticky tape
White paper

1 Cover each flashlight with a different color of filter. Shine the flashlight with the red filter onto a sheet of white paper.

2 Shine the flashlight with the green filter, so the green light covers the red light. What color do you get?

3 Now shine the flashlight with the blue filter, so its light falls on top of the other two colors. Ask a friend to help you if you need to. What color of light do you get now?

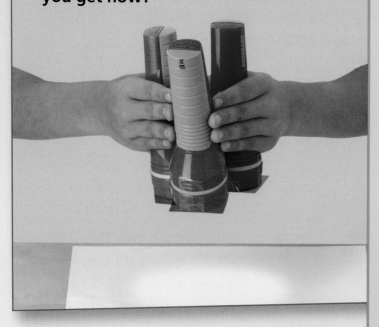

What happened?

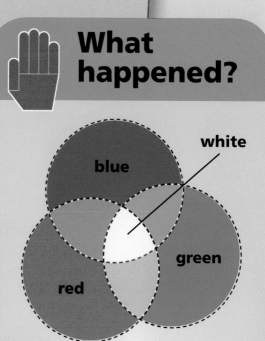

When you shined the green light onto the red light, you should have seen an orange-yellow light. When you shined the blue light on top of it, you should have gotten white light. White light is made up of all the different colors of the **spectrum**.

Theater spotlights

Theater producers use different colored **spotlights** to light the stage. Sometimes they mix colors to make different colors.

Make a Rainbow

In this experiment you will split white light up so you can see the different colors, as in a rainbow.

You will need:
A flashlight
A round black card to cover the face of the flashlight
Sticky tape and scissors
A mirror
A plastic box
White card
Modeling clay
Pitcher of water

1 Cut the black card in half. Stick each half over the front of the flashlight, leaving a narrow slit between the two halves.

2 Pour water into the plastic box until the water is about 1 inch (2.5 cm) deep.

3 Place the mirror in the box, so it is slanted and covered by the water. Hold the mirror in place with modeling clay.

4 Shine the flashlight onto the mirror through the water.

5 Catch the reflection on the white card. Adjust the angle of the mirror and the flashlight until you can see the different colors in the reflection on the paper.

What happened?

Different colors of light travel through water at different speeds. This splits the light up into the colors of the spectrum. The colors are always in the same order: red, orange, yellow, green, blue, and violet. One color merges into the next one.

Rainbows

A rainbow is made when sunlight shines through drops of water. The drops split the light into the separate colors. The biggest rainbows form in the sky, but you may see a rainbow when the sun shines through water from a sprinkler hose.

What Makes the Sky Turn Red?

In broad daylight the sky is blue, except when it is cloudy. When the sun sets and rises, however, the sky looks pink. This experiment produces the same result.

You will need:
A flashlight
A transparent
   plastic box
Water
Milk

1 Fill the box with water.

2 Now add a small amount of milk so that the water turns slightly cloudy. You have added white milk to clear water, but what color is the liquid?

3 Place the flashlight at one end of the box and shine it through the liquid.

Look at the liquid from the other end of the box. What color is it?

4 Look at the box from the side or from above. Can you see the color change gradually from blue to orange-red?

What happened?

As the beam of light hit small particles of milk, the light broke up into different colors. Blue light is easily scattered, so this is the color you see first. The remaining colors combined to give an orange-red light, which carried on to the end of the box.

Sunrise and sunset

The sky looks pink or red at sunrise and sunset. This is because the sun's rays pass through air that is close to the ground where there are more particles to scatter the light. By the time the light reaches you, most of the blue light has been scattered by the particles, leaving the reddish light.

Glossary

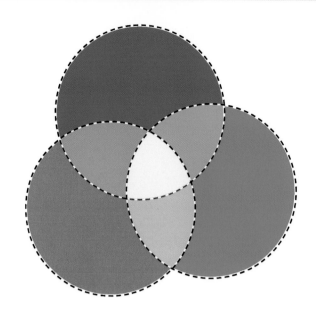

batteries objects that contain chemicals that react to generate electricity.

bulb a glass globe that produces electric light.

device something designed for a particular purpose.

electricity a form of energy which can be used to produce light, heat, motion, and other things.

filters devices that allow part of something to pass through, but block the rest of it. A colored filter allows only light of that color to pass through it.

reflect to bounce light back.

reflector something that reflects light.

shadows areas that are less well lit than the surrounding areas. A shadow is produced when a beam of light is blocked by an object.

spectrum the band of colors that together make up white light.

spelunkers people who explore tunnels and caves deep underground.

spotlights lamps that shine strong beams of light on small areas.

Further Information

Websites

**www.chromebattery.com/battery-kids/projects/
build-a-flashlight**
Website offers instructions for building your own flashlight
using fairly common household objects.

**www.exploratorium.edu/snacks/water_sphere_lens/
index.html**
Make a lens and magnifying glass with a glass bowl and water.

**www.stevespanglerscience.com/lab/experiments/
homemade-kaleidoscope**
Using common objects, build a kaleidoscope that creates a rainbow of colors.

Note to parents and teachers: The publisher has made every effort to ensure that these
websites are suitable for children. However, due to the nature of the Internet, we strongly
advise the supervision of web access by a responsible adult.

Books

**The Illuminating World of Light with Max Axiom, Super Scientist (Graphic
Science) by Emily Sohn and Nick Derington,** Graphic Library, 2007

Light Makes Colors by Jennifer Boothroyd, Lerner Publications, 2014

Light (Science Slam: Fun-Damental Experiments) by Ellen Lawrence, Bearport
Publishing, 2014

Index

batteries 6, 7, 8, 9

beams of light 10, 11

bending light 18, 19

bouncing light 16, 17

bulbs, electric 6, 7, 8, 9

circuits, electric 8, 9

colored light 20–27

cycle lamps 7

electricity 6, 7, 8, 9

fiber optics 19

film projector 11

filters 20, 21, 22, 23

firefighters 17

headlamp 6

LED flashlights 7

rainbows 24–25

reflections 16–17, 19, 25

reflectors 17

shadows 7, 12, 15

spectrum 23, 25

spelunkers 6

splitting light 24–27

spotlights 23

stage lighting 21, 23

sun 15, 25, 26, 27

sunrise 26, 27

sunset 26, 27

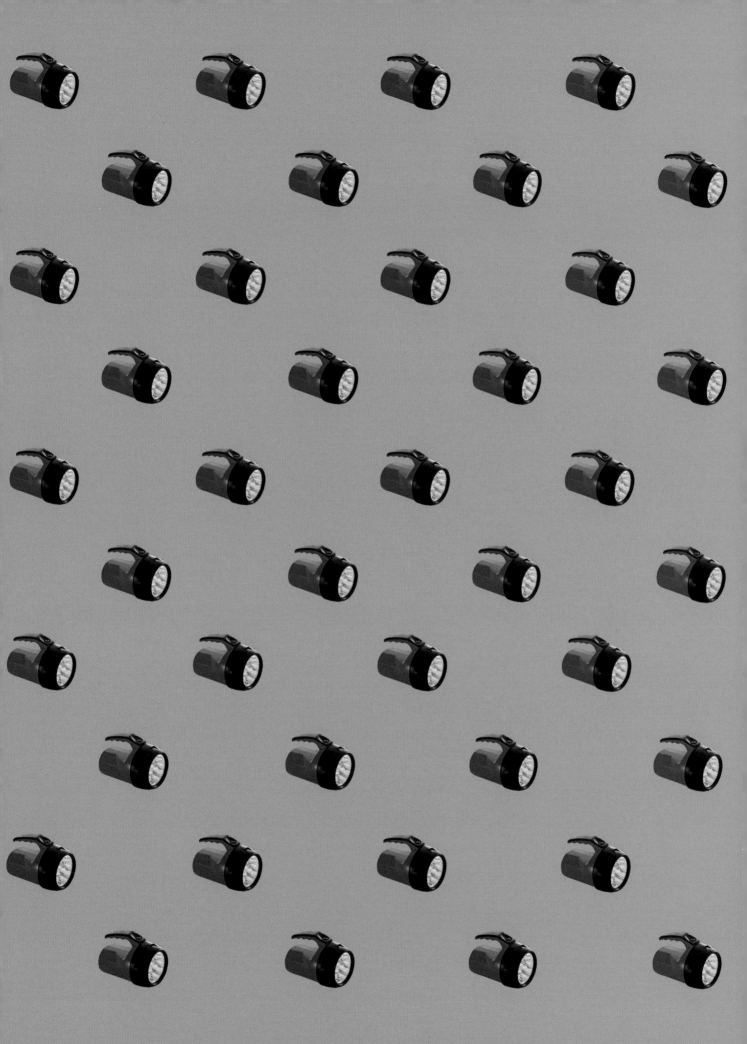